I·N·S·I·D·E
WEST GERMANY

Ian James

Photography: Chris Fairclough

Franklin Watts

London · New York · Sydney · Toronto

CONTENTS

© 1988 Franklin Watts
12a Golden Square
London W1

Published in the USA by
Franklin Watts Inc.
387 Park Avenue South
New York, N.Y. 10016

Franklin Watts Australia
14 Mars Road
Lane Cove
NSW 2066

Design: Edward Kinsey
Illustrations: Hayward Art Group

UK ISBN: 0 86313 579 X
US ISBN: 0-531-10641-1
Library of Congress Catalog
Card Number: 88-50363

Phototypeset by Lineage Ltd, Watford
Printed in Belgium

Additional Photographs:
Allsport 19; Zoe Dominic 22;
Chester Fisher 14; Popperfoto 7, 8, 9 (T);
Christa Staedtler 25, 29

Front cover: Chris Fairclough
Back cover: Chris Fairclough

The land

West Germany is a country in north-central Europe. It has two short coastlines. The North Sea coast is on the northwest and the Baltic Sea coast is on the northeast.

Northern Germany is a plain drained by several rivers, including the Ems, the Weser and the Elbe. The river valleys are fertile. But much of northern Germany is heathland. Central Germany is a region of tablelands and low mountains. Rivers, including the Rhine, the country's leading waterway, flow through deep, scenic valleys.

Southwestern Germany includes a beautiful, largely forested upland area called the Black Forest. But most of the south is hilly. In the far south, on the border with Switzerland, lie the snow-capped Bavarian Alps.

Below: **Schleswig-Holstein, West Germany's northernmost state, is low lying.**

Above: **The Bavarian Alps are the highest part of West Germany.**

Left: **Hamburg is a port on the estuary of the River Elbe.**

West Germany's highest point is the Zugspitze in the Bavarian Alps. It is 2,963 m (9,721 ft) above sea level. Many streams flow north from the Alps. They feed the Danube River, which rises in West Germany and flows east through seven countries before it reaches the Black Sea. The Danube is the second longest river in Europe after the Volga River in the U.S.S.R.

Northern Germany has cold winters, with average January temperatures of 0°C (32°F), but summers are warm. The average July temperature in the northern port of Hamburg is 17°C (63°F). The south has colder winters and warmer summers. The average yearly rainfall varies between about 50 cm (20 in) and 100 cm (39 in). Some highlands are wetter.

Below: **The River Rhine starts in Switzerland and then flows through West Germany and the Netherlands. It is a major waterway.**

The people and their history

Most Germans are descendants of ancient tribes, including Franks and Goths. The ancient Romans named these tribes the *Germani*. Germanic armies finally defeated the Romans in AD 486.

For much of its history, Germany was divided into small states. Each state had its own ruler. In the mid-19th century, the prime minister of the state of Prussia, Otto von Bismarck (1815-1898), worked to unite Germany. In 1871, Prussia's king was crowned emperor (*Kaiser*) of united German empire. By the early 20th century, Germany was a major industrial nation. In 1914, Germany, Austria-Hungary and their allies, who were called the Central Powers, were at war with the Allies.

Below: **Prussia defeated France in the Franco-Prussian War (1870-1871). After this war Germany was united under Prussian leadership.**

7

Above: **A German soldier in a trench in World War I. Almost two million German soldiers were killed in the war.**

The Central Powers were defeated in 1918. In the 1920s, Germany suffered severe economic problems. In 1933, the Nazi Party, led by Adolf Hitler (1889-1945), took power. Nazi policies led Germany into World War II. But in 1945, Germany was defeated. Its cities were in ruins.

The country was divided into four occupation zones. The American, British and French zones were joined together to become West Germany in May 1949. The Russian zone remained separate as East Germany.

West Germany is a republic. It is officially called the Federal Republic of Germany. It is divided into 10 states, each of which has a parliament. The central parliament has two houses, the *Bundestag* and the *Bundesrat*.

Right: **Under Adolf Hitler, leader of the Nazi party, Germany conquered much of Europe.**

Below: **The defeat of Nazi Germany in 1945 left the country in ruins.**

Towns and cities

The former capital of Germany, Berlin, was also divided into four occupation zones in 1945. The western zones became West Berlin, while the Russian zone became East Berlin. Although it is surrounded by East Germany, West Berlin is the 11th state of West Germany. It is the largest city in West Germany (see page 14).

West Germany is densely populated. The most crowded area is the Ruhr, an industrial region based on rich coalfields. The Ruhr contains several cities, including Essen and Dortmund. The number of people working on farms has fallen and, by 1985, 86 per cent of West Germans lived in towns and cities. Besides West Berlin, the largest cities are Hamburg, Munich, Cologne, Essen, Frankfurt am Main and Dortmund.

Below: **A village near Heidelberg in southern Germany.**

Above: **Cologne is West Germany's fourth largest city.**

Left: **Frankfurt am Main is a commercial city, with many trade fairs.**

Hamburg is a great port and trading city on the River Elbe. Munich, capital of the state of Bavaria, is a historic city, but it has set up many industries since 1945. Many publishing and film companies are based there, together with factories that make cars, chemicals and beer. Cologne is an inland port on the River Rhine. It is an industrial and a trading city. Essen and Dortmund are also industrial cities, while Frankfurt is the leading financial and commercial city.

The capital of West Germany is Bonn. Before 1945, it was a small university town on the river Rhine. It became capital in 1949 and, by 1985, it had a population of 292,600.

Above: **An open-air market in the city of Munich.**

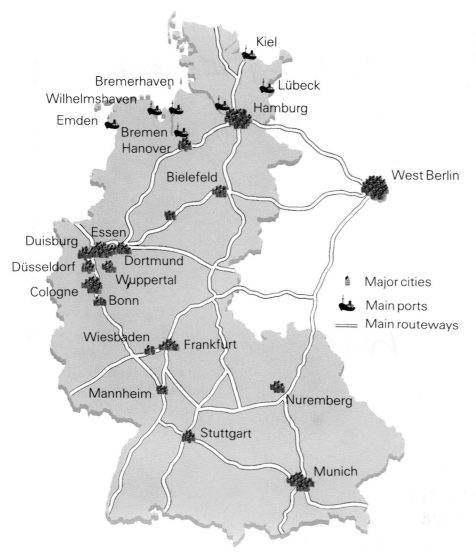

Left: **The map shows major routes and cities in Germany.**

Kiel

Bremerhaven
Wilhelmshaven
Emden
Bremen
Hanover

Lübeck

Hamburg

Bielefeld

West Berlin

Duisburg
Düsseldorf
Cologne

Essen
Dortmund
Wuppertal
Bonn

𝄢 Major cities

⛴ Main ports

══ Main routeways

Wiesbaden
Frankfurt

Mannheim

Nuremberg

Stuttgart

Munich

Left: **Bonn is the Capital of West Germany.**

13

West Berlin is a state of West Germany and it has its own elected parliament. But the Allies (the Americans, British and French), who keep soldiers in West Berlin, have the final authority for governing the city.

Since 1961, a 42-km (26-mile) long wall has separated West and East Berlin, which is the capital of East Germany. The East Germans built this wall to stop people from leaving East Germany. But since 1961, many East Germans have been killed trying to cross the wall. West Berliners can visit East Berlin. But East Germans are seldom allowed to visit the West.

Berlin was badly damaged in World War II. The ruined Kaiser Wilhelm Memorial Church, a war memorial, overlooks the city's main street, called the Kurfürstendamm. West Berlin is a cultural and industrial city.

Below: **The Brandenburg Gate used to be the crossing point between West and East Berlin. It now stands just inside East Berlin behind the Wall.**

Family life

West Germans are among the world's most prosperous people and living standards are high. The average life expectancy is 75 years, as compared with 70 years in 1965.

About 10 per cent of families own their homes, but home ownership is increasing. About half of the people live in houses and half in apartments. Because the average family size is small, most homes are also small and compact. They are well furnished and have at least one television set and a refrigerator.

West Germans work, on average, just over 40 hours a week. Many factories are open at 7 AM and schools by 8 AM. As a result, most families have left home by 7.30 AM. Most schools close between 12 noon and 1 PM. Children return home to do their homework, play or watch television.

Below: **A modern family house in southern Germany.**

Above: **Most German homes are well furnished and decorated.**

Left: **Germans have become much more casual in dress and outlook in recent years.**

Food

Because most people leave home early, breakfast is a light meal consisting of bread, butter and jam with coffee. Lunch is usually the main cooked meal, while dinner is often a cold snack with cooked meats, sausage, cheese and bread.

Lunch may consist of pork or veal with vegetables, *Sauerkraut* (pickled cabbage) is a popular vegetable. Soups are also popular. West Germany is famous for its cheeses and sausages, including Bierwurst, Bratwurst and Frankfurters. Another well-known dish is Black Forest Cake. Apple juice, beer and wine may be drunk with meals. Many German cities now have Italian, Greek and Turkish restaurants. They have been opened by people who came to Germany to find jobs.

Below: **A supermarket in the state of Baden-Württenberg, in the southwestern corner of the country.**

Above: **Breakfast consists of rolls with jam or cheese. There is coffee or milk to drink.**

Left: **Bread and cold meats, with beer or wine, make a typical evening meal.**

Sports and pastimes

The most popular team sport in West Germany is soccer. Some of the country's clubs, such as Bayern Munich, have become famous around the world. Other major sports are gymnastics, handball, horseback-riding, sailing, shooting, skiing and swimming. Jogging is an important way of keeping fit for people who live in the cities. One out of evey four West Germans belongs to a sports club, or *Verein*. Most villages have their own sports club whose members meet once a week.

Many people take hiking trips or use bicycles to explore the country's beautiful forests and mountains. They carry their belongings in knapsacks. Youth hostels provide accommodation for some people. Others prefer to spend the nights outdoors.

Below: **Soccer is West Germany's leading spectator sport.**

Television viewing is a popular pastime in the home. There are three television channels. The Germans are also great readers. Gardening is another leading activity. Some people without gardens rent plots of land, called allotments, on the outskirts of the cities.

By law, West Germans are allowed three weeks vacations each year. Most people have four or five weeks. Many people take their holidays abroad. In winter, many people go to the Alps for winter sports, including skiing. In summer, people travel south. Popular destinations include Italy, Austria, Spain, France and Yugoslavia. Fairs and festivals, such as the beer festival held every October in Munich, also attract many people.

Above: **The beach at Travemünde, a resort on the Baltic Sea Coast.**

The arts

Germany has made great contributions to the arts, particularly music. Great composers include Johann Sebastian Bach (1685-1750), Ludwig van Beethoven (1770-1827), Felix Mendelssohn (1809-1847) and Richard Wagner (1813-1883).

Leading writers include the poet and dramatist Johann Wolfgang von Goethe (1749-1832), author of *Faust*, the playwright Johann Christoph Friedrich von Schiller (1759-1805), and the novelist Thomas Mann (1875-1955), whose books include *Buddenbrooks* and *The Magic Mountain*.

German artists include the painter and engraver Albrecht Dürer (1471-1528). Germany has much magnificent architecture, including cathedrals, castles and other buildings.

Below: **Cologne's magnificent cathedral seen across the Rhine at night.**

Above: **A scene from Wagner's opera *Die Meistersinger*.**

Left: **An engraving called *Knight Death and the Devil* by Albrecht Durer.**

Farming

Nearly half of West Germany is used to grow crops or graze farm animals. Forests cover another fifth of the land.

Farming employs only six per cent of workers, but most farms use modern machines and yields are high. Wheat, barley and sugar beet are major crops. Fruit and vegetables are also important. Grapes for wine-making are grown in vineyards on sunny slopes in the warm valleys of the Rhine and Mosel (or Moselle) river. Cattle are reared on the coastal plains and in the foothills of the Alps. Pigs, poultry and sheep are kept by many farmers.

West Germany produces about three-quarters of the food it needs. The rest is imported.

Below: **Many small farms are still family owned and run.**

Left: **Vineyards on the banks of the Mosel River.**

Below: **Hay-making in the northern state of Schleswig-Holstein, one of the country's major farming regions.**

Industry

West Germany is the world's fourth most important industrial nation, after the United States, the U.S.S.R. and Japan. Industry employs 44 per cent of the workers.

Coal is the country's main resource and it is used to produce most of the country's electricity supply. The largest coalfields are in the Ruhr region. But most of the metals needed for the country's industries are imported.

After the U.S.S.R., West Germany is Europe's leading steel producer. It is the third leading producer of cars after the United States and Japan. Well-known car manufacturers include Audi, BMW, Mercedes and Volkswagen. Steel is also used to make industrial and farm machinery, ships and tools.

Below: **A BMW car plant in the city of Munich.**

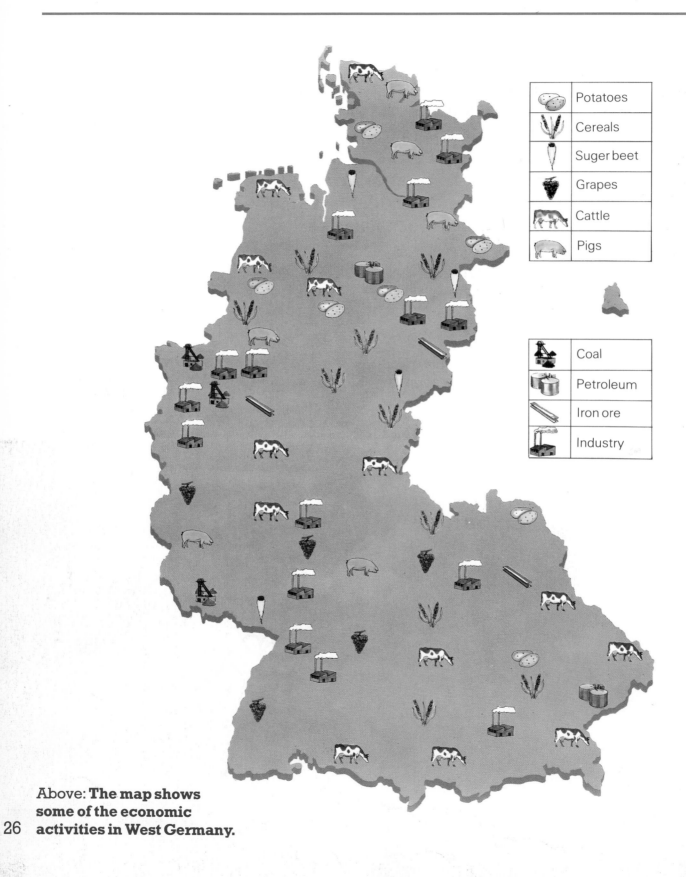

	Potatoes
	Cereals
	Suger beet
	Grapes
	Cattle
	Pigs

	Coal
	Petroleum
	Iron ore
	Industry

Above: The map shows some of the economic activities in West Germany.

The chemical industry is even more important than the car industry. Its many varied products include cosmetics, medicines and plastics. Other products include domestic items, such as television receivers and hi-fi equipment, while high-technology industries produce computers. Textiles are important, as also are such traditional manufactures as china, glass and precision instruments.

Manufactured goods make up 85 per cent of West Germany's exports. Nearly half of its trade is with countries in the European Economic Community (EEC). West Germany was a founding member of the EEC in 1957. This organization has helped West Germany to increase its trade.

Below: **The Kiel Canal, linking the Baltic and North seas, passes through industrial areas.**

Looking to the future

After 1945, with aid from the United States West Germany rebuilt its shattered economy. Its recovery during the 1950s was so quick that it was called an "economic miracle". But the hope that the two Germanies would soon be reunited was not achieved. For years, relations between them were bad. They improved in the 1970s, but no one expects the two countries to be reunited in the near future.

The success of German industry has brought problems. Industrial wastes and smoke from factories and power stations have caused serious pollution. Rivers, lakes and forests have been affected. Many young people are joining groups, such as the Green party, which are working to prevent pollution and protect the environment.

Below: **Education played an important part in West Germany's "economic miracle".**

After its defeats in two World Wars, West Germany has become a respected member of the Western world. It has played a major role in European affairs, especially through the leadership it has offered in the European Economic Community.

West Germans are proud of their achievements. Some people object to foreign influences, including the popularity of American and British pop music among young people. But Germany's great classical composers remain as popular as ever. Similarly, although many young people wear American jeans, many others wear traditional German clothes. Most West Germans enjoy the mixture of the new and the old, which typifies modern West Germany culture.

Below: **Mining and manufacturing have made West Germany rich, but they have also caused pollution.**

Facts about West Germany

Area:
248,577 sq km
(95,976 sq miles)

Population:
60,989,000

Capital:
Bonn

Largest cities:
West Berlin (1,852,700)
Hamburg (1,585,900)
Munich (1,266,100)
Cologne (919,300)
Essen (622,000)
Frankfurt am Main
  (598,000)
Dortmund (575,200)

Official language:
German

Religion:
Christianity (about 49
per cent are Protestants
and 45 per cent are
Roman Catholics.)

Main exports:
Manufactures, including
machines and tools,
chemicals, motor
vehicles and iron and
steel products.

Units of currency:
Mark

West Germany compared with other countries

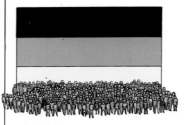

West Germany 247 per sq. km.

USA 26 per sq. km.

Australia 2 per sq. km.

Britain 232 per sq. km.

Above: **How many people?
West Germany is very
heavily populated.**

Below: **How large? West
Germany's land area is
small compared with some
other countries.**

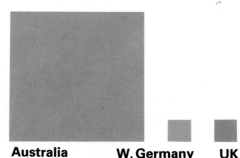

| USA | | Australia | W. Germany | UK |

Below: **Some West Germany
money and stamps. The
Mark is divided into 100
pfennigs.**

DENMARK

North Sea

Frisian Islands

Flensburg

Kiel

Lübeck

Hamburg

Baltic Sea

R. Weser

Lüneburg Heath

Bremen

N

POLAND

THE NETHERLANDS

Münster

Bielefeld

Hanover

Brunswick

West
Berlin

East
Berlin

R. Elbe

WEST GERMANY
(FEDERAL REPUBLIC OF GERMANY)

Harz Mountains

EAST GERMANY
(GERMAN DEMOCRATIC REPUBLIC)

Duisburg

Dortmund

Essen

R. Ruhr

Düsseldorf

Cologne

Aachen

Bonn

R. Rhine

BELGIUM

Taunus Mountains

R. Moselle

Frankfurt

Wiesbaden

R. Main

LUXEMBOURG

CZECHOSLOVAKIA

Mannheim

Nuremburg

R. Neckar

Bohemian Forest

Karlsruhe

R. Danube

FRANCE

Stuttgart

R. Isar

Black Forest

R. Inn

Augsburg

0   20   40   60   80 miles

Munich

0   40   80   120 km

Scale: 1:2,500,000

Freiburg

Salzburg

AUSTRIA

SWITZERLAND

Alps

Index